NOTTINGHAM'S GAS BUSES

SCOTT POOLE

First published 2022

Amberley Publishing
The Hill, Stroud
Gloucestershire, GL5 4EP

www.amberley-books.com

Copyright © Scott Poole, 2022

The right of Scott Poole to be identified as the Author of this work has been asserted in accordance with the Copyrights, Designs and Patents Act 1988.

ISBN 978 1 3981 0675 8 (print)
ISBN 978 1 3981 0676 5 (ebook)

All rights reserved. No part of this book may be reprinted or reproduced or utilised in any form or by any electronic, mechanical or other means, now known or hereafter invented, including photocopying and recording, or in any information storage or retrieval system, without the permission in writing from the Publishers.

British Library Cataloguing in Publication Data.
A catalogue record for this book is available from the British Library.

Orgination by Amberley Publishing.
Printed in the UK.

Contents

Acknowledgements	4
Nottingham Gas Buses	5
401–404 Green Line Route 6, City to Edwalton	8
405–409 Green Line Route 10/10c, City to Ruddington/Rushcliffe Country Park	11
410–417 Red Line 44, City to Gedling	14
418–425 Lilac Line 24/25, City to Carlton, Westdale Lane and Arnold	18
426–433 Generic-liveried Vehicles Used Across the Network of Services	22
434–441 Sky Blue Line, City to Gedling via Mapperley	26
442–453 Orange Line Route 36, City University–Chilwell	30
454–462 Brown Line Route 17, City to Bulwell	36
463–468 Lilac Line Route 27, City to Carlton	41
469–477 Purple Line Route 89, City to Rise Park	44
478–485 Pink Line Route 28, City to Bilborough	49
487–491 Navy Blue Line Route 49, City to Queens Drive Park-and-Ride to Boots	54
492–499 and 501 Lime Line Route 58, City to Arnold Killisick Terminus	57
502–512 Yellow Line Route 68/69/68A/69A, City to Bulwell and Snape Wood	62
513–520 Turquoise Line Route 77, City to Strelley, Flamstead Road	68
500 – The 100th Gas Bus	72
Interior views, Rear End Adverts and the Initial Go2 Network	74

Acknowledgements

I would like to thank all the drivers form Nottingham City Transport for allowing me to take photographs of the buses they are driving. I would also like to thank Anthony Caver Smith for the brief and highly informative depot visit on 7 July 2017 to see the gas station and the fuel station. I would also like to thank fellow photographer Ash Hammond for getting me out of a situation, covering the vehicles I had not yet photographed. Many thanks Ash. I will take this opportunity to also give thanks to Connor, Philip, Fraser, Sarah, Nikki, and all at Amberley Publishing, for this unique chance to write on a subject of my choice.

I will dedicate this book to everyone who has worked so hard through 2020, missing out on the social events, family and friends because of the pandemic.

Nottingham Gas Buses

The search for a new fleet of environmentally friendly buses began with a trial of three Scania Saloon vehicles, using a Bio-Ethanol fuel, during 2008. The total cost for the buses and fuel installation – £520,000 – was secured by Nottingham City Council (NCC) via a bid to the East Midlands Development Agency. NCC are responsible for the implementation, formal monitoring, and evaluation of the trial. On-going additional running costs were funded by Nottingham City Council, with the fuel station assembled within the Lower Parliament Street bus depot. The three ethanol buses in the NCT fleet generated annual savings in CO_2 emissions of 258 tons. The impact of the trial on Nottingham was a reduction in CO_2 emissions of 774 tons. The route chosen for the trial was the number 30 service, City to Wollaton Vale, which was reviewed during the trial. The buses carried over 1.3 million passengers more 390,000 miles during the trial. There was little difference in overall usage, but a slightly higher level of usage than other similar routes on the network. The three buses were adapted to use the E95 Ethanal fuel, which at the time cost £1.21 per litre compared to £0.98 for a litre of diesel. These vehicles would cost around £20,000 per annum to run, but with some £25,000 also spent on the fuel. Although the trial was in some terms successful, it was considered too expensive to be viable for an entire fleet of vehicles.

306 is seen operating out of service on 10 June 2013, still in full Eco-link branding and livery, working with the Bio-Ethanol fuel. After the whole trial was completed all three Scania vehicles were converted back to diesel fuel and were later sold after service with Nottingham City Transport.

As growth for newer environmentally friendly buses grew, hybrid vehicles were purchased by several fleets, including TfL tendered services. The trials with Hydrogen fuel integral Mercedes-Benz Citaro saloons began in 2003, followed by the batch of Wright Pulsar-bodied DAF saloons later during 2013. Two integral Vanhool saloons were added in London in 2017. Around the same time, a trial batch of Vanhool integral Hydrogen saloons worked in Aberdeen with First and Stagecoach. Optare designed and built their own electric range of the Versa and Solo chassis, with power packs placed into a module arrangement. The Metrocity saloon and Metrodecker, both integral vehicles, were also included into the electric range. By far the biggest influence in the UK industry is the partnership between ADL and BYD (Europe), with more than 200 saloon and double-deck examples being used in London, and double-deck examples also in Birmingham, Coventry and Manchester.

Scania, who decided against making a Hybrid chassis, looked at building a chassis that could be powered by compressed natural gas (CNG). The K270 chassis was devised and built, and ADL built a stylish Enviro 300 body using this test/demonstration chassis. By the time of Birmingham's 2014 Bus Expo, a chassis was displayed along with an artist impression of a batch of K270s ordered by Reading Transport and forty in Sunderland for Stagecoach North East. It was also around this time that ADL were completing the finishing touches to the new major model change (MMC) for the E400 and the E200 bodywork styles. In 2016 the first bio-gas prototype double-deck N280UD, with gas tanks situated in the stairwell and above the rear seats in the lower saloon, was complete.

A trial bus was used on the Citylink 2 park and ride service: Victoria Park, City via the Racecourse. The Racecourse site had 470 spaces with full CCTV and dedicated spaces for families and disabled drivers.

The double-deck N280UD chassis was developed as Reading Transport expressed interest in purchasing a batch of gas-powered double-deckers. Nottingham City Transport also expressed interest in the chassis and worked in partnership with Nottingham City Council, Scania, Alexander Dennis and RoadGas, with part-funding from OLEV (Office of Low Emission Vehicles). Nottingham City Transport bid for additional funding for the first batch of fifty-three new gas buses, with the new stylish E400D MMC City style of bodywork, which allowed for an increase of gas pressure in the tanks to 250bar.

During 2013, seen on 10 June, Nottingham trialed this smartly styled Scania K270 chassis with the ADL E300D bodywork with the gas canisters hidden from view. With the addition of the roof canopy to allow an aerodynamic appearance to the whole profile of the roofline of the bus.

The new buses were officially launched in the Old Market Square on a rather damp and cool day in May 2017. Five of the new vehicles were there, with an example in each of the line colours seen alongside Nottingham employees, Scania representatives and local dignitaries. Shortly after the initial launch, in July 2017 the first vehicles were placed into service on the Edwalton 6 on the green line Bridgford Bus routes. Buses 401 to 404 and generic-livered 426 and 427 were in service on the very first day. With a little assistance from Antony Caver Smith, the gentleman behind NCT's publicity for the fleet, a short behind the scenes look at the gas station was organised via social media – huge thanks to Antony for allowing the visit. The gas station is built within the bus depot along with the gas pumps. The pumps work just like a petrol pump, with a fast delivery. The gas is paid for in quarterly segments, as NCT pays for the gas from the grid network at a set price. The gas station was also able to be extended, with another sixty-seven vehicles ordered for delivery in 2018/19. 401–453 arrived in 2017/8 for the Green 6/10, Red line 44, Sky blue line 45, lilac line 24/25 and the orange line 36. 2019 saw the arrival of the second batch of gas buses, 454–499 and 501–520, which worked on the brown line 17, lilac line 27, purple line 89, lime green line 58, turquoise line 77 and yellow line 68/69.

With the arrival of the 120 gas buses, and the additional batch of Euro IV ADL E20Ds towards the end of 2019 for the 5, 7 and 9 green line services, Nottingham was able to finally withdraw vehicles that pre-dated those with 2010 plates. Among these is the last Optare-bodied East Lancashire Omnidekka-styled ScaniaN239UD to be built and placed into service, number 931 (YT61 FFU). This means Nottingham has one of the youngest fleets in the country, alongside Blackpool Transport.

A pump at the gas station.

401–404 Green Line Route 6, City to Edwalton

On 7 July 2017, the first full day of service on the number 6 Greenline route to Edwalton commenced, using buses 401–4 and generic-liveried vehicles 426 and 427.

401 (YP17 UFA) is seen travelling along Alford Road, not in service, travelling to the Wellin Lane, Edwalton terminus. The Bridgford Bus logo is seen along the windscreen base, which sees service 59 linking Trent Bridge with the city and a parade of shops on central avenue. The 6 Edwalton route has a fifteen-minute frequency and a journey time of thirty minutes from the Victoria Centre to Edwalton. On the network of services, the green line buses service the city centre every five minutes.

Nottingham's Gas Buses

402 (YP17 UFB) is paused on Angel Row in the city centre, working the service on 7 July 2017, collecting passengers for Edwalton. The rear destination display shows off one of the features of the new buses – USB power – as specially commissioned adverts reveal the environmental credentials of the Scania N280UD CNG bus chassis, along with the route branding for the number 6 service.

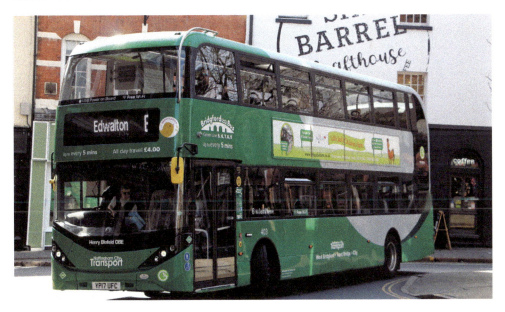

'Well, my dear old things, how delightful to see this bus named after. Our Henry.' Yes indeed it is, my dear old thing. Here, bus 403 (YP17 UFC) is seen on 18 April 2017 working the Edwalton service turning into George Street during the second test of the 2017 England v South Africa series at Trent Bridge, where South Africa won by 340 runs. Henry Blofeld, a long-established member of the BBC TMS team, was retiring after the 2017 series. It was arranged for the bus to be presented during one of the intervals, and Henry was photographed with 403 outside of Trent Bridge. A fitting tribute to a very enjoyable member of the *Test Match Special* team.

404 (YP17 UFD) is seen on Wellin Lane, just setting off for a return trip into Nottingham during the first day of operation. The area in Edwalton offers many pleasant photographic opportunities along the route. The line colours had commenced in 2001, as new buses were delivered to Nottingham City Transport. Scania N94UDs with Omnidekka bodywork, built by East Lancashire in Blackburn, came in 2004. The Go2 network saw the new branding and line colours arrive, with green line buses in an overall white livery with green front ends. Naturally the services saw passenger growth and newer buses arrived during 2010/1, with the final examples of the Omnidekka built by Optare. In 2014 the Scania N230UD chassis arrived with ADL E40D bodywork, to replace older buses. This led to the partnership with ADL, Road Gas, Nottinghamshire Council, Scania and NCT for the first fifty-three gas buses.

Nottingham's Gas Buses 11

405–409 Green Line Route 10/10c, City to Ruddington/Rushcliffe Country Park

405 (YP17 UFE) is parked up and on display at the Grand Central Railway open day on 16 July 2017, next to 161 (OTV 161), a Park Royal-bodied AEC Regent III new in 1954. 405 was used to show off the new fleet of gas buses to visitors and locals who were visiting the preserved railway and the Rushcliffe Country Park.

406 (YP17 UFK) is seen working the 10C on 16 July 2017, the first day the CNG vehicles were used on this Sunday extension to the Rushcliffe Country Park, the home of the Grand Central Railway and its collection of preserved buses, trucks and trains. Here 406 is turning towards the main stop in Ruddington Green.

407 (YP17 UFL) is seen parked up at the 10C Sunday extension stop at the Rushcliffe Country Park, letting passengers off. However, if you look behind the rear wheels you will notice a pool of liquid. The duty engineer was dispatched to investigate. 407 had to be taken out of service to check out the problem, which led to bus 428 (YP17 UFS), a generic-liveried gas bus, taking up 407's duties.

Nottingham's Gas Buses 13

408 (YP17 UFM) is seen on Loughborough Road commencing a return journey to Nottingham during the first day of operation on the 10C for the gas buses. The 10C location offers many countryside photograph opportunities, such as at Rushcliffe and in Ruddington.

409 (YP17 UFN) negotiates the roundabout at Rushcliffe Country Park while working the 10C, adding some modern variety as the Grand Central Railway was also having a running day using vintage and veteran buses. Using vehicles with local connections and a London RT, the local buses included Atlantean 666 ARC 666T, the unique Northern Counties-bodied bus; Midland General Bristol VRT 332 FRB 211H, which was visiting from the Wythall Transport Museum; a Trent ECW-bodied Atlantean; a Barton Plaxton-bodied Leyland Leopard; and an ECW-bodied Bristol MW from the Midland General fleet.

410–417 Red Line 44, City to Gedling

410 (YP17 UFG) turns round from King Street into Queen Street, beginning another run towards Gedling and Wollaton Avenue. The bus also has one of the specially commissioned side adverts promoting the environmental qualities of the gas buses. This batch of buses 410–7 were used from 2 August 2017 on the 44 service, replacing older East Lancashire Omnidekka-bodied Scania vehicles.

411 (YP17 UGC) is seen on Lower Parliament Street on 16 September 2019, working the now extended route serving the racecourse park-and-ride, then forward to Gedling. The changes were made following NCT winning the park-and-ride contract from another operator. The new alterations commenced on 1 September 2019. 411 has the additional park-and-ride branding plus a side advert promoting the new park-and-ride extension.

Nottingham City Transport wanted to engage with children and educate them about the gas buses working in the fleet. With this in mind, the company chose one gas bus to be decorated on the lower front dash with a smile and eye lashes. 412 (YP17 UGD) became *Greta the Gas Bus* during the early stages of 2018. The bus is seen here on 24 May 2019, turning into Gedling main road from Manor Road while working the 44 route.

2 August 2017 saw more of the new gas buses enter into service. Here, 413 (YP17 UGE) is seen working the return journey on the red line 44 on Besecar Avenue before turning on to Arnold Road.

The Gedling area of Nottingham offers some very pleasant surroundings, with many shops and public houses. Here 414 (YP17 UGF) passes the Gedling Inn while working back to Nottingham during a visit to the city on 2 August 2017.

415 (YP17 UGC) is depicted exiting Besscar Avenue on to Arnold Road in full red line 44 route branding. Along with Bio-Gas CNG and Nottingham logos around the vehicle, the new livery was introduced with the new gas buses in 2017. Nottingham have continued to use Scania vehicles since the late 1980s, with demonstrators and the new N113DRB chassis from the 1990s.

Gas bus 416 (YP17 UGH) is seen taking the tight turn from Wollaton Avenue into Besscar Road, seen during a visit to Nottingham on 2 August 2017. The red line 44 was the third route to have these new environmentally friendly vehicles introduced. At the time the day travel ticket cost £3.70, allowing for a full day of travel around the Nottingham network.

Taking the left turn from Arnold Road into Shelford Road is bus number 417 (YP17 UGJ), working the 44 on 2 August 2017. To the right of the bus are the new houses being erected, which are on the edge of Gedling Country Park. As with most of the gas buses, the correct route branding and other decals are placed around the bus. The advert panels would soon be occupied.

418–425 Lilac Line 24/25, City to Carlton, Westdale Lane and Arnold

The lilac line 24/25 became the fourth route to have the new gas buses introduced during the summer of 2017. Here 418 (YP17 UFH) is seen working the route on 26 March 2018, turning out of Digby Lane to Westdale Lane East.

The very busy junction of Westdale Lane and Main Road heading towards Gedling is the setting for this shot of 419, exiting Westdale Lane. Seen working the 25 back into Nottingham on 24 May 2019 during the afternoon rush hour. The neat styling of the E40DMMC City bodywork allows for better application of external adverts on these vehicles.

Westdale Lane East is a long road with many points where a good shot of the buses working the lilac line 24/25 routes could be captured. Here, 420 is seen working the service on 26 March 2018, without the advert panels being filled.

Also seen working on 26 March 2018 is bus 421, heading towards Arnold, turning from Burton Road to Main Road. This road leads to Gedling and is also used by the 44 service. The 25 will turn in to Westdale Lane East to continue its journey to Arnold.

Bus 422 is seen turning from Westdale Lane West to Holyoake Road while working towards Digby Avenue. It is working the 24 on 26 March 2018. 422 had yet to gain side adverts for the local area.

Nottingham City Centre is a hive of activity, with buses, taxis, trams, cars and goods vehicles all looking for space. Here bus 423 is seen exiting Queen Street to Lower Parliament Street while working the 16.50 service towards Arnold.

The terminus for the 24 and 25 services is King Street in Nottingham city centre. Where the passengers alight, it is a short walk to Market Square. Then onwards to the shops, near the square, or a short walk up to Lower Parliament Street and down to Victoria Centre. Here bus 424 commences another journey towards Arnold during a morning duty on the service.

Bus 425 makes the tight turn from Main Road to Burton Road heading back towards Nottingham, during a March 2018 visit to the city. The gas buses have certainly made their mark in the city and have reduced the operators annual Co_2 emissions, with 121 examples in the fleet.

426–433 Generic-liveried Vehicles Used Across the Network of Services

Bus 426 is named *Albert Ball, VC*, and is seen not in service running along Inham Road. Born in Nottingham, Albert joined the Sherwood Foresters at the outbreak of the First World War and was commissioned as a second lieutenant in October 1914. He transferred to the Royal Flying Corps in 1915 and flew reconnaissance missions before being posted in May to a fighter unit. He accrued many aerial victories, earning three Distinguished Service Orders, the Military Cross and the Victoria Cross. He was the first ace to become a British national hero and was tragically killed in action on 7 May 1917, aged twenty.

The very first day of operation with the gas buses on the 6 City–Edwalton service sees bus 427 lending a hand. Here the bus turns out of Alford Road into Stamford Road, heading back into the city. The generic livery uses a grey base with turquoise and a dark blue sweeping line towards the rear of the bus.

Nottingham's Gas Buses

Bus 428 was placed into service on Sunday 16 July 2017, after number 407 had developed a leak during its maiden voyage on the 10C. 428 is seen arriving at the Green, Ruddington, while taking a return journey into Nottingham. The 10C is a Sunday half-hour service that runs between 9.35 and 16.05 and offers weekday morning peak journeys to Ruddington Business and Country Park.

A sunny afternoon near Netherfield on 26 March 2018 and bus 429 is seen making turn in to Main Road from Westdale Road East, while working the 24 back to Nottingham centre. 429 sports special adverts to promote the new gas bus fleet, with its environmentally friendly credentials. Keen eyes will see the Easter bunny sticker and a revised fares sticker in the windscreen.

Bus 430 is seen working the 28 service on 3 July 2019, moving slowly along Bracebridge Drive, near the local shops. By this stage there were more than eighty gas buses in the fleet, and the last few were about to be released in the autumn of 2019.

Bulwell High Street is the setting for this shot of bus 431, which was helping out on the 17 service during the first day of operation, 17 April 2019. Numbers 454–462 were painted into the brown livery for the Bulwell service, which was first run during 2004 as part of the Go2 network. New Scania double-deckers with East Lancashire bodies were used, with newer vehicles arriving in 2010.

September 2019 saw a new service being introduced, a return for Nottingham to Victoria Retail Park, via the racecourse park-and-ride. NCT won the tender when the contract was up for renewal, which replaced the Ecolink service funded by the city council. Seen on Lower Parliament Street is bus 432 working the 50 to Victoria Park on 16 September 2019.

The last of the generic-livered buses is number 433, which is seen working the 36 Chilwell service from the city. Here the bus is seen turning to Inham Road from Bramcote Lane, during a very pleasant sunny afternoon. Having the spare generic-liveried vehicles allows for continued use of a gas bus on the routes served by the type, though there have been a few instances when older vehicles repainted into the 2017 generic livery have wondered onto a gas bus route.

434–441 Sky Blue Line, City to Gedling via Mapperley

18 April 2018 saw the first of the Sky Blue line gas buses arrive. Number 434 is working the 45 service from Gedling into the city. Here the bus exits Milton Street to Lower Parliament Street, heading for the city terminus in King's Street.

Bus 435 is seen arriving towards the end of the journey from the city to the Gedling turning circle, the terminus of the route. 435 turns to Wollaton Avenue from Shelford Road, heading to the terminus, which is not too far from the parade of shops.

The Wollaton Avenue turning circle offers a nice rural photograph of the buses working the 45 sky blue line service. Here 436 is paused by the driver before commencing the return journey to Nottingham City on a sunny 26 March 2018.

Bus 437 informs potential passengers 'Sorry Not in Service' during the visit to Nottingham on 26 March 2018. The bus is more than likely being used as a short turn, when a bus is taken off service and placed back on the route to ensure the timetable is kept in order. This can also happen when the terminus point has a couple of buses waiting time.

King Street is a very busy part of the city network, with three stops for the red and lilac services. While Queen Street is the place to catch the blue and sky blue services. Here, 438 is turning towards its stop on Queen Street, ready for another trip out to Gedling.

Climbing Shelford Road to join the main Westdale Lane is bus number 439, which has just left the Wollaton Avenue stop a few minutes before. It is seen just before Easter, which is why the sticker on the nearside of the destination display is there. As it was the first day of the new gas buses working the 45, there are no adverts on the vehicles side.

Nottingham's Gas Buses

Bus 440 exits the Wollaton Avenue stop, with the parade of shops and the terminus for the 44 just to the right of the bus. 440 has an Easter bunny sticker, and the bus also advertises the all-day ticket – great value at £4 for an entire day riding the whole Nottingham network.

The last of the batch of gas buses for the 45 Gedling–Mapperley–City service is bus number 441, which is paused at the Wollaton Avenue stop. Nottingham City Transport also use a citywide live system at bus stops with the boxes, like the one shown here, near 441. The boxes give real time bus arrival and departure times, along with the scrolling service information, news and the time.

442–453 Orange Line Route 36, City University–Chilwell

Orange line 36 was the next route to gain the new gas buses, with eight dedicated vehicles being used on the service. Here, bus 442 is seen exiting Milton Street bound for Chilwell on the very sunny morning of 18 April 2018.

At Chilwell there is a pleasant section of the route, which offers some scope for photography as buses wonder around a ring road through an estate. Here bus 443 is seen exiting Field Lane, turning to Bramcote Lane before returning to Beeston, passing Wollaton Park, the QMC, and entering the city centre loop.

Beeston centre in the city offers a transport interchange for the passengers, with service provided by Trent buses or the NET tramway. Here is bus 444, working the 13.50 departure from Beeston, with the area's main shopping complex behind the bus. 444 is seen on 18 April 2018 during a very warm spell of weather.

Sections of Bramcote Lane offer the photographer a semi-rural setting for shots of the buses working this interesting route. Here 445, with a very happy driver at the wheel giving a thumbs up, is seen travelling along Bramcote Lane on 18 April 2018. Nottingham City Transport has the most pleasant and polite drivers, always happy to talk and assist with the best value fares and indulge enthusiasts about the gas buses.

Inham Road offers some great seasonal shots of the 36 service as buses turn in from Bramcote Lane. Here 446 is seen in full sun as it begins to travel along this section of the service, again with rural and semi-rural locations for shots.

Beeston Interchange is the location for this late afternoon shot of 447, waiting time at the lay-off section of the transport hub. Some mid-morning peak services operate into the university campus as the 36U for students living in the area.

Nottingham's Gas Buses

33

The junction of Bramcote Lane and Bramcote Avenue offer chances to capture vehicles on the 36 service. Here bus 448 shows off the line livery well, with side advert, route branding, and useful service information beneath the destination screen. Behind the bus is a local convenience store, useful for keeping hydrated on warm spring days.

Nottingham city centre offers more photography for the enthusiast who likes the busy enviros of the city, with a mixture of buildings and areas. Here, bus 449 is seen making its way to Milton Street stop J4 for the Intu Victoria Centre. The bus is depicted on Shakespeare Street during a visit to the city on 17 April 2019, by which time the 17 Bulwell service had introduced the new gas buses to passengers on that route.

The top end of Cator Lane, which is just off Bramcote Avenue, allows for more of an action shot of the orange line buses. Here, bus 450 works the route on 19 April 2019, with double yellow lines in situ to allow buses to turn reasonably into Cator Lane. The shot also works for the opposite way as buses exit Cator Lane, but it does need a 25-mm lens setting.

Inham Road again sees bus 451 about to head around this section of the route. Even with an overcast period of weather, the standout orange livery really catches the eye with its vibrant colour.

Here is the same location seen in the shot of bus 448, as bus 452 turns in to Bramcote Avenue from Bramcote Lane. It was taken on 17 April 2019 under cloudy skies; the orange livery stands out to brighten the location.

The final shot of the orange line vehicles is bus 453, which is seen in the best location for nearside turning shots: Angel Row, Nottingham. The side advert panels, which formed a ridged to keep adverts within the section, work well on these buses. The day ticket price had also increased by April 2019 to £4.20, which is still great value if out all day on the buses.

454–462 Brown Line Route 17, City to Bulwell

Bulwell is a vibrant area of the city, with plenty of shops, pubs and cafes. It also has a busy bus station. Here is bus 454 working the roundabout into Carey Road on the morning of 17 April 2019, the first week of operation of gas buses on the brown line 17 service.

Did I mention the pubs in Bulwell? Well, as luck would have it, the Red Lion on the high street offers a great photo opportunity for the photographer. Here, bus 455 is seen passing the pathway near the pub. The idea for this shot came from Ash Hammond, a local enthusiast.

Bus 456 is seen turning into Main Street from Bulwell High Street while working the morning journeys on the 17 service. With a different light, the brown livery does has a distinctively dark chocolate look to it.

As with the other Nottingham services, the 17 Bulwell route offers many locations for shots of the buses working the routes. Here bus 457, with its happy driver at the wheel, passes along St Albans Road before arriving into Bulwell town centre.

The turn in to Kersall Drive from St Albans Road again offers great seasonal photography, as bus 458 shows in this shot taken on 17 April 2019. This particular location also works in the reverse as buses turn in to St Albans Road.

Hucknall Road roundabout, near the city hospital, with Valley Road to the right of the bus. Seen negotiating the roundabout is number 459, working back into Nottingham during the midday period of 17 April 2019. The new fleet of gas buses have provided a much needed increase in passengers from around the city; the public seem quite happy with their new transport vehicles.

Hucknall Road, again with bus 460 seen exiting Kersall Drive in to what is quite a busy bus route road, with the 17 and buses from Trent and Stagecoach also using this road.

During a 3 July 2019 visit to Nottingham, there was enough time to capture a shot of 461, working the 17 Bulwell service. A return to the Kersall Drive/St Albans Road corner offers this view of the bus heading back into Nottingham.

The final bus of the batch dedicated to the brown line 17 Bulwell service, bus 462 is on the high street in the town commencing a return to Nottingham. Like all the Nottingham routes, the Bulwell route offers town centre, high street, residential, semi-rural and city centre locations.

463–468 Lilac Line Route 27, City to Carlton

The terminus for the 27 Carlton service has a small turning crescent to allow vehicles to reach the Elmhurst Avenue stop on Coningswath Road. Here, bus 463, the first of the batch of six buses used on this lilac line route, is seen on 24 May 2019.

Cavendish Road with Carlton Hill/Burton Road behind the bus is the location for this shot. Bus 464 is making its way towards the terminus for the 27 service on a very pleasant day in May 2019.

Carlton Hill is on the route of the lilac line routes 24, 25, 26 and 27, with the new 26 Pathfinder service replacing an old number with improved buses. Working its way up Carlton Hill is bus 465, complete with specially commissioned adverts for the gas buses.

Bus 466 is seen turning into the city centre terminus point for the lilac line routes on King Street, which is one of many smaller interchange hubs within Nottingham city centre. This shot was taken on 16 September 2019, your author's last visit to the city before the 2020 lockdown of the UK due to the worldwide pandemic.

Seen travelling up Coningswath Road on 24 May 2019, at around ten past three in the afternoon, is bus 467, which is just a small distance from the turning crescent where the bus will turn into the road and pause at the bus stop.

The final bus of this batch is number 468, which is seen working the 27 during 24 May 2019. Here the bus is turning into Carlton Hill having just completed a run along Lower Parliament Street, city centre loop for the service.

469–477 Purple Line Route 89, City to Rise Park

3 July 2019 saw the first of a new batch of vehicles for the gas bus rollout for the Rise Park 89 service. Many enthusiasts and Nottingham residents will remember the former Go2 stop at Trinity Square way back in 2004 for 89 service, when the East Lancashire-bodied Tridents worked the 89. Here bus 469 basks in the July sun before setting off from the now Lower Parliament Street bus stop for the Rise Park service.

On 25 May 2019, bus 470 is seen wondering near the Belsay Road stop while travelling along Beckhampton Road. On this particular day, the gas buses were joined by some of the Scania diesel vehicles on the route, as the gas buses were being phased into service.

Nottingham city centre at around 10.47 in the morning on 25 May 2019. Bus 471 is seen arriving towards the terminus. The bus is seen turning off South Sherwood Street into Lower Parliament Street, just a hop away from King Street and close to stop P5 for the 89 service.

The 2018 UK Bus Awards saw many of the individuals working for the industry getting awards and recognition for their hard work and dedication. Nottingham City driver Arron Johnson was awarded the accolade of the 'UKs Top Bus Driver 2018'. Arron's usual beat is the 89 service. Following his award, bus 472 has a rear advert and his name on the bus. When the photo was taken, Arron's name was yet to be added to the front.

3 July 2019, yet another beautiful day. Bus 473 is seen turning to Milton Street having just commenced another journey on the 89. After a few days in service, the buses would gain the side adverts for promotion and information for Nottingham BID, a local organisation that arranged events and special shows across the year.

Beckhampton Road, in the area of Bestwood in Nottingham, is the location for this shot of bus 474, seen on 25 May 2019. The Bestwood Park is to the left of the bus, with a wildlife reserve also in the park, allowing for the visitors to explore and listen to the local wildlife.

Rise Park bus station/terminus also services the brown line routes 15 and 16, as well as turquoise line route 79, towards Arnold. Here bus 475 is parked as the driver takes a few minutes away from the bus before departure. Rise Park terminus also has a parade of shops and cafes for the passenger to enjoy.

In the full blaze of the sun at around 17.10, on 3 July 2019, bus 476 is seen exiting Beckhampton Road to Bestwood Drive. From here, 476 will take a few minutes to reach the Rise Park terminus, just clipping the Top Valley area of the city while the bus sports an advert for Coventry University! Strange, as Nottingham has universities as well.

Mansfield Road is a very busy mix of areas, with shopping parades, a bus depot, and various bus routes going along the road. For Nottingham, it services the 56, 57, 57X, 58 and 59 lime line services and the 87, 88, 89 and 89A purple line routes. Trent Barton's Calverton service and Stagecoach's Pronto service, which serves Mansfield and Nottingham and extends to Chesterfield, also stop here.

Seen on Mansfield Road at 16.20 on 3 July 2019 is the final bus in the batch for the 89 service, number 477. The bus had yet to gain the promotional side adverts, but it has the route branding and additional passenger information above and below the destination display. During 2021, 477 was repainted into the generic livery and has been used across the network.

478–485 Pink Line Route 28, City to Bilborough

During the summer of 2019, the 28 pink line service to Bilborough was next to be given the new gas buses. Here the first of the batch, bus 478, is seen turning to Birchover Road from Cockington Road, just after 12.30 in the afternoon.

Canning Circus is another great place for photographing buses running around the Nottingham area, as both NCT and Trent buses use this area heading out of the city. Here, bus 479 is seen approaching Ilkeston Road while working the 14.00 town centre–Victoria centre–J6 stop departure on 3 July 2019.

Strelley Road is the location for this shot of bus 480, which is not in service at the time. Vehicles on most routes can be short turned and return to a timed point along a route to keep up with the timetable, especially at peak times. In some cases, vehicles have caught up during a busy time at the terminus and one bus is taken out of service again to keep the timetable running to time.

The Bilborough terminus area is the location for this shot of bus 481, which has just commenced a return trip to Nottingham and the popular Victoria Centre. The 28 service terminates on Stotfield Road in a pleasant estate area of the city.

Here turning in to Wigman Road is bus 482, working the 28 service on 16 September 2019. 482 has just left Bracebridge Road, and a park, the Harvey Hadden complex and a local high school can also be seen.

Bus number 483 is seen arriving at Bracebridge Drive having turned in from Wigman Road, while working the service on 16 September 2019. As in the picture of 482, the Harvey Hadden sports complex is behind the bus, offering many health and fitness benefits to the local community.

On 3 July 2019, at around 12.45 in the afternoon, bus number 484 is seen turning into Stotfield Road from Cockington Road. During a fabulous spell of warm sunny weather for the area, 484 will continue along this road until reaching the terminus for the service.

Bus 485 is seen turning in to Bracebridge Drive from Wigman Road during the day on 3 July 2019. The park behind the bus is busy with locals enjoying the school holidays in the sunny weather.

Bus number 486 is seen on the 3 July 2019. As the new buses were settling into their new roles, 484 is seen on Birchover Road heading towards the terminus of the 28 service on Stotfield Road.

487–491 Navy Blue Line Route 49, City to Queens Drive Park-and-Ride to Boots

In 2019, the 49 navy line gained five new gas buses as the park-and-ride on Queens Drive was awarded to NCT after a successful tender for this service. Here one of the five buses, number 487, turns in to Angel Row working the service on 3 July 2019, with full adverts for the park-and-ride service.

The tramway lines on Market Street sees bus 488 turning in to Angel Row, passing the now pedestrianised Long Row. The 49 service goes around the city loop, passing the major passenger interchange areas. 488 sports adverts for the park-and-ride plus route branding.

Bus 489 is seen turning out of George Street to Lower Parliament Street during a warm spell of sunny weather on 3 July 2019. The new buses have a fifteen-minute headway, with all five buses working the route.

The area of George Street sees all the green, orange, turquoise and navy line routes pass through to get to Lower Parliament Street. Here, bus 490 turns off Carlton Street to George Street and stop H8 before setting off around the centre and back to Boots and the park-and-ride.

Lower Parliament Street is an area where all 120 gas buses can be seen, working the various routes around the city. Routes from George Street, Milton Street and the lower part of Parliament Street all pass through, as do the services which terminate on King and Queen Street.

Here, bus 491 is seen on Lower Parliament Street passing the main shopping area and the Victoria Centre as it works the 49 navy line service to Boots. The park-and-ride extension was won from Eco-link, a local council service operated on behalf of the city council using electric-powered BYD integral saloons. The new-look navy link route commenced in September 2019, as NCT have also won back the park-and-ride services at Victoria Park and the Racecourse park-and-ride site too.

492–499 and 501 Lime Line Route 58, City to Arnold Killisick Terminus

On a glorious 16 September 2019, bus 492 turns in to Surgeys Lane from Homefield Avenue while working its way back to Arnold and Nottingham. This particular corner would offer an interesting contrast in the autumn as the leaves change colour.

Late afternoon sunshine on 3 October 2019 sees bus number 493 working the 58 back to the city. Here the bus is seen about to run along Church Street, not far from Arnold town centre.

The Gleneagles Drive turning circle and terminus of the 58 service offer different photographic views of the buses on the service. This stop is serviced by the 59, operating via a slightly different route. Here, bus 494 is paused at the terminus before proceeding back into Nottingham on 16 September 2019.

Bus 495 shows just how tight the turn in to Homefield Lane is from Surgeys Lane. The new 2017 livery sits well on all the ADL E400 City-style bodywork, with adverts neatly placed into the panels, allowing the livery and branding for the routes to standout.

Another shot from early October 2019, as bus number 496 is seen working an afternoon diagram of the 58 service. Again, the bus is seen about to turn into Church Street from Surgeys Lane, heading for the city.

After a few minutes break, allowing the driver to stretch their legs, buses leave the Gleneagles terminus, turning into Killisick Road. Here, bus 497 is departing the terminus at 11.13 as it begins its journey back to Nottingham via Arnold.

The 58 service, along with all the other routes in Nottingham, offers the bus enthusiast many useful locations and pleasant areas to photograph the Nottingham City Transport fleet. Rural, residential and city locations offer changing environments for the shot. Here, bus 498 is seen travelling down Birchfield Road heading towards the 58 terminus during a visit on 16 September 2019.

Bus number 499 is seen working the 58 on the same day as 498 in the previous image. Here the bus is climbing the hill section on Birchfield Road before turning into Homefield Avenue.

Killisick Road sees bus number 501 working along the 58 route, heading back to Nottingham. Most of the new services offer a seven-minute frequency, allowing for a good service throughout the day, with a twenty-minute frequency during the evening as buses run until 23.20. There are three late night N58s on Fridays and Saturdays.

502–512 Yellow Line Route 68/69/68A/69A, City to Bulwell and Snape Wood

An exceptionally sunny and bright 3 October 2019, as bus 502 works the 68/69 route on Seller's Wood Drive, going off service during the morning.

Bulwell Main Street, at the junction of Revenswood Road, sees bus number 503 turning towards the bus station. The bright yellow livery really stands out and catches the eye as these vehicles work the route. 503 was yet to gain side adverts when this shot was taken.

The Snape Wood turning circle and terminus of both the 68/69 service, along with the 68A and 69A variations, offers a good view of the rear end of the new gas buses. The 2017 livery is shown to good effect in this shot. The Bio-Gas logo and route branding can also be seen here. The gas tanks are hidden underneath the rear window and under the stairs of these vehicles.

The junction of Hoewood Road and Seller's Wood Drive offer turning shots of the new gas buses, as can be seen here. 505 turns in to Hoewood Road while working a mid-morning duty on the 68 back towards Bulwell and Nottingham.

Milton Street in Nottingham, 4 October 2019. Stop T4 is the location of 506, which is not in service. (Ash Hammond)

The changing colours of autumn are clear in this shot of bus number 507 working the 69 service. The destination screen shows the line colour and the new payment method of contactless cards. Seen on Hempshill Lane. (Ash Hammond)

Bulwell is the location for this shot of 508, working the service back to Nottingham city centre. The bus has turned in to Highbury Road and will pass Basford before passing Nottingham College and then heading to the city centre.

A twilight shot of bus number 509 at the Snape Wood terminus, as dusk turns to night on 5 October 2019. (Ash Hammond)

On 3 October 2019, bus 510 is seen exiting Hoewood Road into Ravenswood Road, continuing its morning duty on the 68 service.

Bulwell bus station is the location for this shot of bus number 511, seen paused at the stop before heading back into the city. Bulwell has plenty of local transport links to and from the city, including the 17, 35, 68, 69, 70, 71 and the 79 group of services. With the NET tramway and a railway station, Bulwell residents have plenty of transport options.

My final shot of the 68/69 section is this one of the last batch, bus number 512. It is seen travelling along Snape Wood Road during the morning of 3 October 2019.

513–520 Turquoise Line Route 77, City to Strelley, Flamstead Road

The last route to gain the new gas buses was the 77 to Strelley on the turquoise line, which ventures to Flamstead Road. Bus number 513 turns at the roundabout on Moor Road before turning to Flamstead Road while working the service on 3 October 2019.

The Moor Road junction with Strelley Road offers a nice location for turning shots of the 77 route vehicles. Here bus 514 is seen working the route on 16 September 2019 during the busy afternoon period when the schools finish for the day.

Another good location for shots of the Strelley gas buses is this particular junction on the Strelley Road and Aspley Lane area. Here, bus 515 is seen working during the afternoon of 16 September 2019, looking very smartly turned out on the service.

On the opposite side of the Strelley Road and Moor Road junction, heading towards the Asda supermarket in Strelley, bus number 516 is seen exiting Moor Road bound for Nottingham while working the turquoise line service on 16 September 2019.

The roundabout at Flamstead Road sees bus number 517 departing for the city loop on the 77. Again on 16 September 2019, the fresh looking vehicle works the service. The side adverts are yet to be added to the bus.

1 October 2019 is the date of this shot of bus 518, working the 77 as the bus returns to Nottingham. The bus is seen near the Bluecoat school as it pauses on Aspley Lane. (Ash Hammond)

Nottingham city centre sees bus number 519 operating the 16.17 departure from Maid Marion Way, stop M4. Here the bus is passing King Street as it ventures towards Strelley on 20 November 2019. (Ash Hammond)

Bus 520 is seen on Alfreton Road on 31 October 2019. With the final deliveries and entry into revenue-earning service, the new gas buses have been enjoyed by passengers and NCT staff. The launch in May 2017 drew national media interest and was a hit with the Nottingham public. (Ash Hammond)

500 – The 100th Gas Bus

The 100th gas bus to be built by ADL was exhibited at Euro Bus Expo 2018, held at the NEC, Birmingham. Here the bus is on the Scania stand, with plenty of interest surrounding the vehicle. Inside the bus had Nottingham-style seats. It would eventually become number 500 in the NCT fleet.

After undergoing several demonstration duties, Nottingham finally got DD18 GAS into the fleet, with its pleasant overall advert celebrating its status as the 100th Enviro 400 CBG city bus. Here the vehicle is seen working the 28 Bilborough service on a bright and sunny 15 June 2020. (Ash Hammond)

During the later stages of 2020, Nottingham decided to give bus 500 a new overall advert/wrap to advertise the virtues and credentials of the whole gas bus fleet in the style of the initial NCT promotions for gas buses. Seen here working the 24 Westdale Road–Digby Avenue service. (Ash Hammond)

Interior Views, Rear End Adverts and the Initial Go2 Network

The gas bus's glazed staircase offers more natural light in to the bus, which improves passenger safety. Here, on 7 July 2017, one of the buses has specially designed interior posters and information about the fifty-three new vehicles arriving.

The rear upper saloon shows the different approach to the seating arrangement for these new buses. The gas tanks are behind the fibreglass mouldings for the seats. The seats also have USB charging sockets for mobile devices, allowing a boost charge for the passenger.

The lower deck seating arrangement is interesting, as the low floor section is dedicated to wheelchairs, parents with buggies, and elderly passengers. The offside has more seats, along with the raised rear section. The advert at the back shows the environmental benefits of the new buses, reducing harmful particles each year.

The buggy zone is on the nearside of the lower saloon, with two handrails that offer support for the parent maneuvering their child in the buggy. The zone is designed to allow two buggies with parent seated near child.

Following recommendations after a legal case in West Yorkshire regarding a wheelchair user, buses can now have a dedicated wheelchair zone. With the ADL City-style body, the zone is clutter-free, allowing for good maneuverability of the wheelchair.

Five of the seats within the lower saloon are made a priority for elderly travelers, who often enjoy the freedom a bus pass brings to their day. These seats also have USB sockets, so everyone's favourite grandparent can charge their phone and listen to the latest sounds. The lower saloon pictures were taken during the author's brief and informative depot visit.

Nottingham's Gas Buses

The upper saloon seating arrangements allows a pleasant environment for travel, with large windows, the glazed staircase, and few handrails offering a largely clutter-free area. Along with improved leg room, there are the free WiFi and USB charging sockets and two information screens with route details, advertisements and a NCT video all about the new fleet.

Looking down the lower deck of 412, working the 44 Gedling service as it pauses at the Wollaton Avenue stop. Compare the seats with the depot shot of the lower saloon on page 75. The seats have a different headrest in this picture, and the information screen is located in the staircase bulkhead. Thanks to the driver of 412 for allowing some pictures to be taken.

Bus and route information are delivered in screens on both saloons. Here the lower saloon screen is located in the staircase bulkhead. It displays the time, route bus stops – in this case the 24 to Digby Avenue – and bus stopping sign. Video and still pictures are also displayed on the screens. 26 March 2018.

The upper saloon monitor is placed at the stop of the stairs, where the whole saloon can see the screen. Again, as with the picture above, the same information can be seen, with the addition of the route number. These screens also allow passengers to view the CCTV cameras onboard – sometimes you see someone waving. Audio announcing next stop announcements also assist passengers who are distracted. 26 March 2018.

Nottingham's Gas Buses

Bus advertising has helped boost the revenue of operators across the years. This particular advert caught the eye with the gangster grandma pose used to advertise carpets. 404 sports the advert while working the 6 Edwalton service on 7 July 2017.

Bus 406 advertises the bane of all buses – the car. Here it is on George Street working the number 10 service, running along the city loop. The rear advert sells the whole package of service, sales and spare parts for a local Mercedes-Benz franchise in the city. The side advert shows the Ruddington Motor Company, a specialist pre-owned vehicles seller.

Johnsons & Partners can sell your home for less than 0.5 per cent, according to the advert placed on bus number 414. Standing opposite the parade of shops on Wollaton Avenue in Gedling, at the terminus for the 44 service.

A novel way to advertise your services are to place the advert like a lonely-hearts column in the paper. Here bus 422 sports an advert for David James, who are looking for properties in the area of the route 24. The bus is seen approaching journey's end as it nears Digby Avenue.

Nottingham's Gas Buses

Here seen on the back of bus 436 is an advert for an online site selling bespoke furniture – a simple advert. 436 is paused at the turning circle at Wollaton Avenue on a bright and sunny day.

On the look-out for a stylish conservatory? Well you're in luck as bus 452 advertise such a service while on the 36 service. 452 is seen on Cator Lane turning towards the Chilwell loop, just off Bramcote Avenue.

Bus 426 is named *Albert Ball, VC* and has a different rear end panel, remembering those Nottingham heroes who fought in both world wars. It's a fitting tribute to those who gave their lives for the freedoms everyone has today. 426 is seen on the Chilwell loop while working the 36 service.

Here Express Lettings advertise their services, which include a 9 per cent fee, as bus 454 wonders up Kersall Drive while on the 17 Bulwell service.

Nottingham's Gas Buses

Nottingham bus drivers have performed well across the years, as evidenced by the recent Bus Driver of the Year accolade offered by the UK Bus Awards. Here Jatinder Kumar is depicted on the rear of 464, working what is the driver's regular route. Nottingham has won the very prestigious Bus Operator of the Year award five times in recent years.

Nottingham did very well at the 2018 awards, with some category nominations leading to wins. Here bus number 472 sports the 2018 Driver of the Year, Nottingham's Arron Johnson, with the man in question driving the bus. These particular rear adverts also give the company that personal touch, serving the community and giving the driver more personality in the eyes of travellers.

As previously mentioned, September 2019 saw some changes to the operation of the park-and-ride site within the Nottingham city area. The navy line buses 487–491 are featured on pages 74–76. Here on Angle Row is bus 491, with full rear and side adverts along with route branding for the 49 Queens Drive park-and-ride.

Bus 494 is seen at the 58 Gleneagles Drive terminus with another local letting agents advert. This time Holden Copley show off successful clients' thoughts on the service, plus an array of accreditations and awards.

Bus 410 shows the standard rear end layout, with advert panel on the bonnet and route branding where the lower deck window would normally go. Featured here is an NCT special advert for the gas bus fleet.

In this final section, the focus is on the Go2 network, introduced by Nottingham City Transport as it sought to reverse the decline in passengers numbers in recent years. The high frequency Go2 network used colours and routes placed into sections, for easier passenger options. Here bus 427, an East Lancashire-bodied Dennis Trident, is seen on Queen Street working the 44 service during 2002.

Beastmarket sees another Dennis Trident with East Lancashire bodywork on 48 navy line service to Clifton. The livery was white with the line colour at the front of the vehicle. The network was a successful move by Nottingham – during the first year, a rise of 1.5 per cent passengers was achieved. The message was getting through.

Nottingham's Gas Buses

With the success of the new network, Nottingham again turned to Scania for its double-deck orders for 2003. These integral vehicles had polish designed bodies but were constructed at the East Lancashire factory in Blackburn. Bus 723 is seen approaching the then Trinity Square terminus of the 17 Bulwell service on 1 August 2004.

One of the new 2004 deliveries was another batch of Scania/East Lancashire vehicles, here 743 is paused on Trinity Square on 1 August 2004. This area of the city is now pedestrianised as vehicle are using stops on Lower Parliament Street or Milton Street, thus forming the city loop for buses.

The continued growth with the new network saw the introduction of a new red line route – the 43 to Bakersfield. Here bus 902 pulls away from Queen Street working the 14.17 departure to the area on 12 June 2012. This bus was part of a large order for fifty-six buses to be delivered during 2011, and would be the last East Lancashire-bodied buses delivered to Nottingham.

Investment continued in to 2014, with an order for forty new integral ADL E400D, which arrived during the spring of 2014. Here bus 617 is seen turning to George Street fresh to the Strelley service. More similar double-deckers followed in 2015 in order to improve the fleet profile. The next stage was the purchase of the 120 bio-gas double-deckers from 2017.

Bus 955 was repainted during 2014 to celebrate the centenary of West Bridgford Urban District Council and the motor bus serving the area. Here the bus, smartly turned out in the livery, is seen on Angel Row heading for Edwalton on the 6.

During 2016 Nottingham also celebrated the fitieth anniversary of the last trolley buses serving the city. The final routes were the 36 and 37, serving the city centre and running along Mansfield and Nottingham roads. This ended thirty-seven years of operation from 1927 until 1966. Here bus 676 is seen departing the 2016 Sandtoft Gathering while been displayed for the day; after withdrawal from the fleet, a local group of enthusiasts ensured 676 was donated to the Nottingham Heritage Vehicles group.

The generic-liveried vehicles do some work across the network during the week. Here bus 426 is seen working the 44 to Gedling, running along the main Gedling Road past the Co-op and Westdale Lane. 426 is seen on 26 March 2018, still carrying its special bio-gas adverts.

Bus 427 is about to continue along the city loop, here turning to Carlton Street from Fletcher Gate while working the 6 service. The bus was seen during the first day of operation of the gas buses on the 6 City–Edwalton service. A nice touch is the Bridgford Bus sign in the destination display.

Another of the generic-liveried buses working the 44 Gedling service is bus 428, passing through the Gedling area on 2 August 2018.

Tram tracks and the overhead wires clearly show that bus number 429 is within the city centre of Nottingham. Here the bus, seen on the 36 Chilwell service, is passing the pedestrianised Long Row as it turns into Angel Row.

17 April 2019 and bus number 430 is working the 10 to Ruddington, a pleasant village on the Loughborough Road.

Bus 431, seen here on 26 March 2018, is working the purple line 89 Rise Park service, just over a year before the gas buses were allocated to the route. The bus is turning to Milton Street from Lower Parliament Street. It also has a sticker reminding potential passenger there are revised fares in operation.

A fine spring day in a suburban setting on 18 April 2018. Bus number 432 works the 36 service. the bus is seen Bramcote Lane after going round the Chilwell loop, before returning to the city.

September 2019 saw a new service commence in Nottingham, with another contract win for NCT. This time the former Victoria Park Centre and the park-and-ride service, which had been won by Ecolink and run by Nottingham Community Transport from 2014. NCT won the service back after the route was put out to tender. Here bus 433 is on Lower Parliament Street on 16 September 2019, working the new route.

Seen here in glorious sunshine is the number 404, seen at the Edwalton terminus of the 6 service. 404 has the full route branding along with Bridgford Bus's logo in the destination display and around the bus.

The third route to gain the exciting new gas buses was the red line 44 to Gedling. Here 415 makes a turn from King Street to Queen Street. The bus is seen on 2 August 2017, during the first morning of service along the route.

Nottingham's Gas Buses

Hot on the heels of red line 44 was the introduction of the gas buses for the 24/25 lilac line services. Here 421 is seen on 26 March 2018, working towards Arnold on the 25 service, turning away from the King Street city centre terminus.

Bulwell High Street is the location for this shot of bus number 462, the last member of the batch of vehicles for use on the brown line 17 service. Seen during the first morning of the introduction of gas buses on the route, 17 April 2019.

To conclude this book, two of your authors favourite shots of the new gas buses. A preferred city centre location is the junction with George Street and Carlton Street, which allows for a pleasant turning shot – as demonstrated by bus 514 working the 77 to Strelley on 16 September 2019.

Here bus 474 turns into Beckhampton Road from Bestwood Park Drive during the morning of 24 May 2019. The gas buses were joined by two Optare/East Lancs-bodied Scania N series deckers.